Song of the Line

Song of the Line

Poems by Jack G. Gilbert

Engravings by Henryk Fantazos

Introduction by Annie Dillard

A 2007 HORSE & BUGGY PRESS BOOK

with appreciation to
Jerry Tarver and Katherine Smith

SONG OF THE LINE

©2007 all poems Jack G. Gilbert
©2007 all images Henryk Fantazos
©2007 Introduction, Annie Dillard

First Edition
ISBN 978-1-60402-616-0

401-B1 Foster Street
Durham, North Carolina 27701
www.horseandbuggypress.com

Table of Contents

Introduction by Annie Dillard

P O E M S

ENGRAVINGS

Introduction

ANNIE DILLARD

Look!

A medley of work by two fine artist friends:

—Laconic and odd poems by Jack G. Gilbert, who has published literary studies on Jonathan Swift and Edmund Waller.

—Rare and ingenious engravings by the master artist Henryk Fantazos, who has won prizes at exhibitions across America.

They are neighbors of ours in Hillsborough, North Carolina. Artist Henryk is a gift to us from the Polish Nation and the great traditions of painting from 1400 to 1900. After becoming a citizen of the USA in 1975, he has lived in West Virginia and in North Carolina. His mastery stems from curiosity about and knowledge of the natural world, of philosophy, and of literature. The extent of his creativity in painting and graphics can be seen on his website: fantazos.com.

Poet Jack is a Texan, who grew up in Louisiana, and taught there for some years before retreating from the academic life to North Carolina to live with his wife Colleen their own version of five acres and independence.

If art proves anything, one might say that this collection proves that art is fun, eccentricity abounds, love is complicated, good things exist. Henryk and Jack are artists in the school of Dürer and Horace.

A Heaviness of Heart Remembers

A heaviness of heart remembers
a gladness of a song.

The words of dawn like embers
keep warm hope all night long.

Enchantment it is, is not,
and dancing, somewhat,

the simple in it, underheard,
beckons in a whispered word
of love incurred.

Brother Lawrence Lotto

Since I won the lottery
all women in one way or another are pretty
and the men all in another or the same way witty.
The skies are not always blue
but the blue of the skies always is;
people snarls and tangles
turn out to be friendship;
filling and emptying my purse
is like singing well to myself
a song the composer hears approvingly.

As for my health
in the opinion of the best doctors
I am lucky to be alive.

I invest heavily in plain and accidental things
and at night sleep dreamful tight,
too well served to fret
and having (in these lines) given it all away.

Haunting

When our ghosts are introduced to one another
wafted on soft air of jasmine
we'll touch wings, touch wings, touch wings
and bounce like Spring Azure butterflies
quick to stop into oneness
and disappear the while

Tightrope Walker

The tightrope walker never slows
for eye-rhyme equilibrium,
his only trick to force the balance
when it's likeliest away,
whether over bank or missus
or this or next week's precipice.

Life Class

And not just at the start
you were in every way desirable
to talk and eat and sleep with
to see and touch and kiss.

Together we skipped a season
to join mellow autumn with green spring
and all was pumpkins and blushing pears
and apple blossoms
and perfect pink dawns
time after (not enough) time.

Steadily, steadily a stingy hand
has scraped away the Botticelli
for a flat place
to sketch a minimal winter.

Yet real ghosts are
beneath the bare and bloodless,
silvery ripe, forms we see and know.

Under

Nietzsche likely objects
to a roughing
from one of his own
and the bondage of
a life or wandering calisthenics
set to monster music,
while in the operetta
at the real end
of a wild century,
superman has had his day
and we ask what's after
when over is over.

A modest ideal person,
adequate to human life,
with the vitamin virtues
courage and temperance and thrift,
so the world goes
slower or faster or ends,
an old man in underwear
atop a crumbling building
stares at
the remarkably hard ground.

Weeding

Let's hope German Chancellor Kohl
sometimes leaves affairs of state
to stay at home to weed the cabbage,
joined by all the Atlases
who're holding not the world but offices,
the same day, once a week,
to weed their gardens, out of sight,
all the world at home as nothing's happening,
all politicians, all anchor-men,
the movers and the shakers
and the moved and the shaken,
the mischief makers and the mischief watchers.

And these then unused to solitude
 from habit saying to the weeds they pull,
"Have a good day."

A Potato Couch

The green eye wants to see
in the earth that closes it
tilth that tubers die for,
grass and leaves and wood
digested by world conquerors,
the legless and the millipede
regressing through
the finest guts
of trencherman solicitude
that no pea-size clod distress
Princess Potato's late winter birthing bed.

Don't

on this precipice don't say
"will we fall?"
or "time not to push our luck?"
ask
"will I hold you?"
dream
featherbeds and haystacks
dream
flying
dream
clouds

In the School for Old Men

In the school for old men
the sirens teach.
Not fair to look at
nor seductive
they are strong
and smell of woman.
They wear no clothes at school
and dress their body hair.
Their hands have fine sharp nails
and liquid joints.

With hands alone they teach
and no man can gainsay.
Pages and days of despair
a flutter of fingers
confutes and marks with
arabesque Q.E.D.

Spontaneous suppleness arrests
consciousness wearing down,
as if it were a long life,
a long civilization
that wastes to the core
in false parallel
of green stalks and warm limbs.

Whatever measures thought and gesture
is not time.

Sound of Self

The Flatness of Water

At dawn the lake was smooth,
Old Master smooth.
To the eyes, to the sense of up and down,
and to the mind,
it was flat,
and joyful
to that part of us that is not quite head
and not exactly heart.

The constabulary for the arrest of
epidemic misconceptions and vulgar errors,
well-funded and nearly everywhere,
requires me to renounce this water error
and only write the truth
(which for them is easy)
that the atom itself joins unmatched pieces
and is surely anything but flat,
that the slightest wind or flow of water
makes the surface bend,
which in any case at the edges curls
in a caress of surface tension.
And all waters exist on a sphere,
the oceans themselves part
of a droplet incomplete.

So, they conclude,
water is flat in just the way
that man is rational.
Briefly and not exactly so, if ever,
subject to distortion, rills and bubbles
and undercurrents, with Nietzsches and Rimbauds
of antic rapids and water spouts,
and seen from space, by scientists or angels,
anything but how it seems below.

Unsteady perhaps, yet not illusion,
this water where it can be it is level.
The lake will do to calibrate
my ancient transit.

Old Woman in the Temple

dear lady, whose wrinkles flout
and shrivel out
who totters up
to take the cup

with eye of wren
and shape of dove
legs of doing
breast of love

your doctors treat womanity
do everything but so renew
that growing old
is yet to do

still your resilient mothermind
hale and here right now to find
breakthrough intervention
for God's inattention

Corkscrew

Blacksmithy shop's no place for love,
there's no pretence the world's not rough,
and strong's the stuff--for will
and hard's the stuff--for science
and point's the stuff--for winning.
A polished awl's the tool for power,
      knowing, admiration.

All sufficient awls yet dull and rust
and ones bright and sharp
are known
to thin
to bend
to turn
from heat without and in
and curve
graceful eager and hale
into a helix.

The advantage of their curves
conduces them of use to self
mankind and god, and draws to all
good spirits and companion love.

Bare Ass Affirmation Moon Rising

love is a burden chosen
the energy of the effort
the melody in the racket
the callus of hard helping
full aerobic being in the world

a mambo
in the midst of war and dogma
Sufis monks and dreamers
feet on burning sand
knees on freezing stone

fellow postmoderns, evolved
and actualized,
the floor insured
and airconditioned,
can we dance

Sarabanda

For Nancy, October 3, 1998

I grow old on your birthday
drinking back through years of wine.

In living well
there's wear and tear,
and pleasure may lead to decrepitude,
but if abstinence by itself
could give you vigor
the old folks' homes would empty
from time to time
and then refill,
halfwit inmates claiming
that the fun of being drunk
is being sober after.

So let me start again.
I grow young on your birthday . . .

Moontime

This tardy lover the moon
comes later every evening
each time further into night
until it's day, hurried on
by the impatient robust
never waning sun, metronomic
in his haste.

Imagine instead
the moon defines the day,
as sets the moon rises the sun,
earth turns slower to adjust love's rhythms
to hours set for everything else,
gathering, cooking, fighting, thinking.

All then will be well,
or a little better,
when the moon relaxes
in a night each night of her own.

Identity

(A is A and not B)

Quick you'd have to be
to forgive a neighbor
who elbows through your heart
and takes with his exploding lungs
your own last breath.

In a subway rag bag of body and cloth
bloody and burning
experts will seek facts,

none sharper than my last thought
most correctly dead
no piece of me a murderer.

The wounded at least will see
in the indifference of fragments
a difference of regrets.

7/13/05

What the Fox Knows

sore dream it is
in midst of debate
does the fox know more
than the coyote?
the evidence hard won
pain and patience in smelly places
neither subject cooperates
goes in no straight line
in no place you want to be
and sneaks up your pen to piss
some bad science:
that both know how to fly,
the one before the other after
midnight

and grin like Huck Finn and Sancho Panza
each telephoto snap
(no use videotape, they go in circles
slowly, slowly, and hypnotize the
cameraman)

only so much conclude
the fox outfoxes anglos best

Treasure

Leaping from the chaun tree the leprechaun
begged the farmer for a bit of sotweed
to fill his empty pipe. With care
the farmer passed to him
a leather purse and wooden match.

After a dozen puffs
and reverie of snaps and dragons,
the wee man spoke again
slowly to the farmer, who had begun to stare
in admiration of the gracious smoking,

"The secret of life you can have of me."

The farmer turned more grey and taciturn.
At last he said,
"Can you tell me will it do me any good?"

"Probably not! At this dim moment
they will call it
still another crock of ballocks wisdom."

The News Wakes Us Up

The news wakes us up in charge of the world
(a duty that comes with tuning in)
and we try hard nonetheless to listen,
to remember what hearkening sounds like,
to hear the slow beginning, long middle, and
languorous ending of one breath,
one heartbeat, one sunbeam,
even as an ATF team beats in our front door
screaming about a wave of toxic music
just down the street.

Stillness seeks its own
not to notice is the loathsomest form
of un-solidarity
fingered in a line-up, on our own
and everyone's screen,
our lawyer flashing que cards
advising
"be like a news man
talk shit and act CARING
or your ass is mud."

He is proud of the six-letter word.

Old Man's Beard
(for a namesake poet)

grieve forward each year
into the white fringe blossoms of mid-spring--
a fettuccini of peony--
your own white beard thin and soft--
there's sorrow that though next year and next
you will wait for this gentleness and see it
one year not, not see, not be

grieve forward as well as back
in tearing words
and wearing matter

the soft tassels and old beards hang in spring
in chill wind and warm rain

Ancient Tune

upon the soft earth
of the grave prepared
for the predicted death of our love
we'll practice union
unto perfection
and ourselves the master sextons
we'll inter
boredom and inconstancy

and laugh at the impotence of scoffers
who can barely want
every good thing not to be,
roundness of earth
depth of sky
resonance of conscious life
dart of spirit through all being
love that ever waxes

Mezzo Stato

Where prairie was
where they say once was peace
in air and ground
thunder and whine machines in haste and terror
as of some ghastliness behind
in Gary or Ohio.
Up from land and lake ahead
towers a frantic angularity.
It these contrivances screaming seek,
welded and bolted and strapped together,
metal and rubber and mammal.
In the air dense with fumes and noise
many signs advise
somewhat adjusted frenzy.
And under them rampage on
such endless rows
could I have guessed
birth had undone so many?

Alias Poet

In the universal order
of our Muslim brothers
what will come of a minor poet?
And assuming he will be forthwith dead
what will come
of the name of the minor poet?

Pray to all different
and indifferent gods including Allah
that when no letters are permitted,
but truth about Koran,
that my doubtful doubting name
be the vessel into which
canny to stay alive
the secretly and unfaithfully inspired
tuck their poems,

over time, the gifted the mystic
inner infidels blaming their verse
on me, safely dead, but living
as such a seer, such a poet, such a lover.

Hafizes and Dadus and Khamirs
and Runis and Jacks
tossing their flowers into my urn
by their merit famous without harm
to me or them.

Swamp Preacher

Just Grace

In public parking lots my ancient car
appears aggressive, worn and dented.
Yet it takes me farther than I need to go,
the while suspected of working at being poor
in a rich world.

The fullness of this world
everybody's sure's
a scene god's left to Us,
of Our Comforts and Our Gadgets,
from his one hand
and from the other Our Agendas, whereby,
inside and out the doors of comfy churches,
resurrected collectivists
prod the affluent poor
to call the affluent rich
to reckoning,

a fête of fierce pity
and queer piousness
of harming in the name of soothing
and getting in the guise of giving
and praying this justice:

"Be grateful for what's taken away;
 eat guilt and drink fear;
 god forgive you if he can stand it;
 love each other if you can stand it."

Song for Marsalis

Paint me a jazzy song
around a black and booming bass,
make the colors swirl
in an easy reveling.

Pour the greens from clarinets,
and purples from trombones,
the trumpets always golden,
golden running into red,
and sometimes a saxophone
for blues.

Tell the story one more once,
sadness comforted by music,
the notes the little wings
that bear us
bear us up
and over trouble.

Paint me a jazzy song
around a black and booming bass,
make the colors swirl
in an easy reveling.

Ivied Walls

Summer's end is near
and evening closes doors
on another musty year
of criers and of bores.

Restless starlight wills
through the vaulted windows
re-mote the dust on sills
to statued innuendoes,

The empty rooms of night
embrace a chilling echo
of phantom wrongs to right
and rancid horrors let go.

Yet at end of night as fogs
obscure what has been black
the witched pedagogues
break fast on the fractured fact.

Candles on their own that light
get pricked out by thumbs,
moles of corrected spite
that from central thinking comes.

They yearn for contents, these walls,
for sunshine, for essence,
for a tread that falls
from something as yet sapiens.

Uprooted Home

Real Things

What help when what we
Trow
Will scarcely be remembered

As winds of instant access
Blow
Thicker still the thickly known

Into paradox and
Woe,
Night that falling breaks the day,

While yet the moment's man must
Go
Stunned to pick the pieces up

Left from a planetary
Show
Sponsored by a bellywash?

Euprotes

The first the wisest the unknown
Pre-Socratic Euprotes,
the song-and-dance philosopher,
held the motions of the dance
free the mind to sing in laughter
where wisdom has its only moments.

Contrarily those who straightway think
without preliminaries
torture thoughts like muscles
overwrought and tensed against themselves
and never relax into philosophy,
always per se
graceful, melodious
amusing
and short.

A Petite Potato

The pneumatician's news was that
"The reading is two Pascals,"
I lost the rest of what he said
in calculation
of the odds
of so much mind at once.

Those who watch and count
philosophers
never expected another Aristotle
and are still in recoil from
Aquinas's protracted imitation.

Will another lost in numbers
to the power of Pascal
find his way round O
to one?

Hard the Fall

"It was easier to burn anabaptists than to refute them."
11th Britannica

A monstrous deed
finds a thousand and badly needed excuses
but never the ink
to blot the fact that someone chose to do it.
Hope the herb in the pot of human life
brews a tea of justice for those who wake each day
(and pray not) from one dream into another.

The odds though in the ring of history
so much happens anything may happen
history itself or even justice
eventually and for a moment.

Happen so the challenge of heavyweights
by three amateurs, Dreschel and Storch and Stuebner,*
        against
Luther and Blackdirt and Zwingli and Al.

Nearly 500 year ago
the amateurs did not even know
what the canvass floor of ring,
what the water bucket, what the ropes were for.
For stomping out the brain, for drowning, for
throttling.

If the choice that sudden comes
is cut out the heart of a victim
or offer our own instead
the panic

*Anabaptists who came to see Luther; he had them banned from cities; when
  their doctrines spread they were persecuted by arrest and torture or executed.

44

to speak and write and act as if
any other kind of thing is the case, fate or impotence
or "ourselves the instruments of grace"
or any mindflash that lets us off the cross.

These three men, with their own clear thoughts
about an inward matter, and handicapped
by a habit of consistency,
received their first and last lesson in self-defense
from Luther and Blackdirt and Zwingli and Al.

Today in low German lands no one dies for re-baptism,
for any baptism, or no baptism,
and few would kill for any part of Luther or his church
or be pounded for conscience's sake
into the shit he so frequently invoked.

So this is only justice of the very poor and poetic sort,
by which you are not to imagine,
my simple ones,
you Muenzers and Storches and Stuebners,
shivering in your dressing rooms,
that you will either win or lose
or have it faithfully reported.

Hungry and barefoot, simple and true
is the name of the alley in the city of the world.
Shifty and doubtful, insightful and sad
is the name of the mainstreet in the city of the world.
To Wittenburg thirsty men to talk of clearest water.
To Wittenburg cross men for further crucifixion

Duffy Morel

The Limbs of Winter

The limbs of winter sing
to those who listen,
not the whistle of the cold
not the snap and rattle
of the twigs that sweep and break.
The lullaby comes
from the rippling sinews of
the swaying of the boughs and trunks,
baritone affirmation
of the stoutness
in upstanding.

Discretion

Where lightning strikes the earth in the Sudan
the natives make a pile of stones,
a shrine,
to honor the caressing
of their mother earth.

Once three shrines are built on any spot
they prudently desist
and respect the privacy due
to intense erogenous zones.

Surface Temperature

Distant and strong the sun
facilitates all sorts of fun
and yet so glorious so sunny
it is for sure per se not funny.

Fall

Head over heels
mind too slow body too fast
to do geometry of awkward arcs
of arms and legs.

The center of gyration (me)
fell a good eight feet
into a softish roof of tin.

Sudden gratitude
said the man with a junkyard
is the way
to sudden happiness

and gratitude you'd miss
in a trampoline world
all bouncy ground
and safety nets.

For CB

A rose is not a rose but many,
many strategies of luring,
luring lovers to its blossoms.

A rose is not a rose but many
odors of rare oils and spices,
caresses for a world of noses

A rose is not a rose but many,
many, many sorts of blossoms,
single, double, semi-double
up to cups from A to D,
cabbages with scores of petals
set in quaint topologies.

A rose is not a rose but many
efforts to achieve the balance
of the odor, form and color
of the human female beauty.

A rose is not a rose but many,
many strategies of luring,
luring lovers to its blossoms.

Movement of Roots

Our new grass roots movement
against grass roots movements
is praying for rain
and sunshine—
luckily always enough dirt.

Although what we want
is odd but still inclusive,
we get more signatures
and money then we need,
luckily benefitting from the ill
we mean to cure.

Be aware we say
of other roots,
of weeds, of perennials,
of trees, large and hard to move.

A Rose

A rose knows no ambivalence,
its scent and blossom lure all in,
its thorns and prickles ward them off,
its roots and tendrils hold all tight
and suck them dry.
A rose knows no ambivalence.

Organic Matter

To the undertaker's daughter nine years old
it seemed the dead were filling up the world.
When she helped to curl the hair of those
who were no longer ladies,
their deadness didn't frighten her.
Rather in the modest way of corpses
they kept adding to an already
undeniably desperate oversupply.

She dreamt of them as stacking and stacking and stacking up
embalmed and most of them in coffins
around the towns and cities that she knew
arranged according to their creeds.

There were some Pentecostals and Witnesses,
and many brick-like stacks of Baptists,
her own Methodists sorted by size
and still retaining bits of flowers.
The Presbyterians repeated themselves
in two well-separated bunches,
and she did not know exactly whose
were some garish and highfalutin dead
in pentagons and hexagons of coffins.
They all seemed restlessly thrusting up
about to topple
higher than the courthouse,
filling up the countryside,
nudging the derricks of the oilfields.

This was distressing too;
her father had sunk his money into oil,
a product she was taught in school
of former living things
now become a rich thickness
pumped from the ground.

For months until distracted
by another worry,
she prayed some mighty force
would compress the mounting bodies
into something
precious and useful to life,
like perfume or Coca-Cola.

Another Disaster from El Niño

It rained so much
trout lilies shook their locks with pleasure
and undertook to populate the hillside
and subdue the world
with soft and subtle hues.

Rhymes for Rudyard

A pauper's grave is good enough
for those who've toiled at night,
who've starved to write their music,
who've dared a hopeless fight.

Red beans and rice are food enough
for those who live to work,
who dream and build cathedrals,
who pity them that shirk.

A scrap of cloth is hood enough
for those who brave the seas,
who sail by stars and dance on spars,
who relish every breeze.

Two little sticks are wood enough
for those to make a cross
who live a life gainsaying death,
who find the gain in loss.

A pauper's grave is good enough
for those who've toiled at night,
who've starved to write their music,
who've dared a hopeless fight.

Hunchback's Canoe

Thearion the Baker*

They have a peek at my craft,
these bakers of ideas,
but don't stay put for the hard parts.
They wander away erratic and distrait
that truth may turn out to be
something someone already said,
or something to them
excruciatingly simple,
like
"Keep the working surface clean,"
 or
"It is good to eat."

*See Plato, Gorgias 518

Thearion Again

And quiet is what
they cannot find,
those restless, horny minds,
much less keep,
even though, I swear by these floury hands!
one in three parts wisdom,
and one in two politeness,
is silence.

beatus ille

Wanted: Nearly Dead or Just Alive.
Governments after me
all of them
UN down to county and town,
implacable to arrest my poverty and age.
No posting of my profile in post offices
(lean thinker, distinguished grey),
rather full frontal facts:
"*old,*" "*stubborn, chronic old,*" (not young)
"*rural,*" (no public water, sewer, pavement)
"*occupationally challenged,*" (poet, unknown)
"*subsistence farmer*" (grows peas and arugula)
"*unbalanced*" (from wind and weather).
and "*irreversibly indifferent to
economic competence*"
(that is, not in computers,
or otherwise owner of a moneytree
with automatic climate and robotic harvester
that also does the bank deposits).

Despite governments that want me
to give me money
(taking an alarming amount of it back),
I eke of my own what they let me out
and live easy
with occasional friends and poems,
dapper in fine linen trousers
from Goodwill.

The Beauty Machine

In the twentieth century
Jasper started early,
nearly made it to the end,
in Arkansas, pretty much
like everywhere else as Plato thought
a kind of cave
with rocks and bats
and images on the walls.
He rambled as a boy in fact
through prehistoric caves
where it seemed to him
in Arkansas as well as Avignon
there were bosses of political machines
who kept in caves in darkness
talented neanderthals
to do their portraits.
Though hairy and heavy
and clumsy but smart,
in cunning paleolithic coup,
the bosses resolved to be remembered
as graceful, powerful, and thin.
And because they got their meat by theft
they chose to be depicted
in the act of hunting.

These pictures led old Jasper
when young to his one idea:
the art of politics was to have
leaders in fact the way the artists drew them.
A fair conclusion perhaps
by an explorer of caves
and reader of books,
in a land of missionary desperados,

on a diet of cornflakes and peanut butter,
hamburgers and saltines.
All his money he spent
to print his truth
on the inside covers of books of matches
and on printed sheets
thin enough to slip into Gideon Bibles.

The famous one moment of fame was his
in an interview with a newsman from the Times,
who found him in a long and narrow
clapboard house next to a filling station
at the end of a shadowed hall
behind a door; on the door a sign
'The Beauty Machine.'
Before his editor crossed it out,
the newsman wrote:
'This stag my heart leaps
a swampy ditch
each time I'm not in this hallway
painting politicians."
What the paper printed
was the newsman's baiting Jasper
with a neat and overwhelming picture
of horse-thieves and judases
in Washington.
In reply Jasper read from a letter
posted free to him by his congressman,
a report of good works and kindly thoughts.

Over the decades
Jasper sent
to the leaders of his day
a personal message:
'The beauty of the hunter-leader
is to love his people and to strive
to see them healthy, noble, happy.'
To Mao, Castro, Stalin,
to Daly, Hoffa, Getty, Huey Long,
to Perons, Bushes, Clintons,
and a hundred more.

Some of them replied in letters,
and, to a man and woman,
saluted Jasper for seeing
the sacrifice and purity of motive
in their leadership.

He died in his office,
in Mena, Arkansas,
smiling at the walls
covered with such replies
content
his Beauty Machine was working.

Second Collection

The second blessing of money
is to give it quite away
and in this church
you get a another chance
after main collection
when, near the end,
the basket is passed again,
for a worthy effect.

To work the crowd
for second collection
the crowd sings a hymn
led by an Heldentenor
about the unaccountability
of good actions, dogged truthfulness,
canny justice, and sweaty work in art and life.

The pastor beams:
"make a note on your checks
if you believe
you don't believe a word of it."

The World Is Full of Mercies

The world is full of mercies
and tempered winds
and helping hands

with big bucket bail
and magical ways
to beat the rap

on the net and in the yellow pages
faithfully
cross their palms

The world is full of mercies
and tempered winds
and helping hands.

"New Yorker in Dixie: Talk about Humor"*

The odor of magnolias hung
hazing up the lights
in the lecture hall,
the trees themselves intruding through
the Roman arches of the windows.

The audience in mortarboards
and striped pajamas
tucked their balls and chains
beneath the seats.

Was it really just like that
or an image of a pure deduction
(just as in geology)
no other way to account
for all these people being here
in this climate,
in this room,
and not some other place?

    The man from the magazine
    was there to lecture on
    unstable substance
    humor,
    up Eastern apprehensive lest
    a new form of ignorance
    combust spontaneous
    in magnolia fume,
    or ignited by his own winces

*Peter de Vries once lectured in Louisiana on humor,
a funny man with a straight face; his lecture is
re-imagined in a way that might amuse him.

before and after and (fiercest) during
the academic introduction.
Uncomfortably pinned
between John Updike
and someone
whose name he didn't catch,
hoozit the writer, it seems,
who had discovered on his own
that experience justifies the world,
his experience,
in whatever, in everything,
strange food and drink,
serial marriage, group sex,
Old Uncle Gomorrahy and all.
The bounty of this world
that he could grab
and get away with
all of it,
the perfect heist,
and personal theodicy.

Did the introdouceur
really say all that?
or was it just cologne
one notices on every campus
in the West,
with the usual hint of civet
that the world's redemption ends
in the perfect flushing of each personal commode,
all of us inoculate
against everything
and living to a hundred twelve?

To matter straight and dry he went,
    we laugh
    when the mind is humored
    into little ecstasies,
    at a puzzle solved,
    a prophecy fulfilled,
    a connection seen, a pun,
    pleasure in a point of knowing,
    in discovery, in playing doctor.
    and it works even when
    the puzzle isn't really solved
    or the prophecy is fiddled,
    or when old rivalry
    finds exhilaration in
    a fact of ethnic oddity.

    Of funky metaphysic comes
    a black humor trinity,
    death in charge
    absolute
    doting on
    warm, chirpy Pan
    doing its own thing,
    breeding temporary life,
    and an ironic sprite
    singing at the sickle's edge
    in the play left for the mind
    the cat's pajamas of
    its universe.

Did it there peter out
or was the ending phony
as in a symphony
with more to come?

It was not funny,
not finishing,
and no poet
led him on
to revise the list
of gagsters who missed the cue
(distracted by the shticks
of Caesar or of Sartre)
that gave the world
its comic form,
unbent the wiseguys
into perfect stooges
and in a final stunt on death
gave everyone a punch line.

Lines on the Earth

Contemplating the dirt upon my grave
that had somehow itself
contrived to be inscribed
"This is not work to be envied."
Odd, for I had expected,
"Fear is no way to live."

Both

Mind skinnies out of self
and splashes like a droplet eye
through surface harmonies
into the pool of being
and seeing sees to see suffices.

Though Monarch self bounce rough
neither wear and tear of lacy wings
nor quick and rending death
can quite reverse
accomplished fact
of form and color.

Caitiff

His copper poison for him* aperitif,
the venoms in his eyes suffice
to mortify, never mind a body
all digester muscle four feet long
partway in the creek.

Crosswise in his mouth a fish
he seemed to think at risk
and disbelieved the oath
I didn't envy it at all.

Atremble when past the fish the tongue
flicked down a viper gauntlet,
I backed away
neglectful of courtesy
and glad
that dragons
never were.

*a copperhead

Something Nice

The woodshed full will not admit
any sort of mischief now,
no stinging willow switches
from angry aunts, mothers of cousines
a naughty boy has fondled—
no naked one-time cherubs
caught out in primal play—
no grown-ups taken
in usual tangles
of gladiator strife.

There are no cords to be removed
for pleasure or for whipping,
no room indeed for anything
but cords that count
and can be counted,
neat woodbats row on row,
dry hickory yellow-cream and hefty,
and the lighter southern oak
pastel softly glowing as if already coals
iron-oxide and brick with bits of cinnamon,
anticipating warmth of hearth and heart
of human life
at least as old as guilt.

All Things Considered (1995)

Q. Will you read some verses?
A. When the world was new
in the other direction,
Sanskrit was the highway,
mind-friendly with exact and opulent words.
Like wrappers of cinnamon or myrrh,
the words kept about themselves
the essence of their things.
Shantih for peace.
And less pleasant ones,
like thag, in plain English thug, a word
we've borrowed, having a need.
A happy lingualism it is to dream
that if early on the thags had been destroyed,
the word would never have been
and thugs be rare among us . . .
Q. In verse capital letters, yes,
but capital punishment!
Recall the human progress out of bloodfeud,
remember toleration, tout comprendre c'est
tout pardonner, and don't cast the first stone.
A. They lived by highway robbery.
Q. We're all of us
indifferent honest.
A. And always, on principle, killed their victims.
Q. It is hard to prove intent.
A. In ritual solemn religious strangling.

Q. In fairness one recalls the excesses in history
of Christians and Jews.
A. At understandably peripatetic
ceremonies, the faithful thags
excited themselves like cats with prey
high on a strangling.
Q. Governments should provide deterrents;
good street lighting and education
and crisis centers for the strangled victims.
A. The thags were kind to the old, employed them
as spies for new victims and gave them
best seats at the strangling.
Q. Aha!
A. The sexual pleasure at the garotte
was intense.
Q. Thank God! we can all agree on this,
not to quarrel how you get your nookie.
A. The ending of thugs
is the beginning of civil life;
you cannot say,
"It is we who made the thugs."
Q. What about free speech?
And you are out of time.

Best

Best to live by best advice
"fear no more"
cheer the words
into courage
not expecting
no way hard will happen
but heart full head strong
to live it through
with fellow travailleurs
in friendship

Urbane Conversation

Children!

Loathe to abandon the world
to teens of all ages
the very old, like turtles,
still dare seas too deep
and sands too wide.

Even into the melee of freeways
they drive, strewing at times
carnage
with brittle human
and auto parts.

Sure they could pull over
in courtesy
to let the able disable themselves,
the able who see it this way:
dying old in the road with boots on
is a waste of good boots.

Native Art

In a bud of Eglantine*
the gothic arch
is green and lanceted,
signed with wispy tips
of sepals,
and dotted with tiny hairs.
In the bud La France**
the pomp of Roman arch
and subtleties of ribbing
trick the eye to doubt
the perfect roundness,
In this garden sketchbook for design
lilies kourai line a porch,
sweeps of branches make pagodas,
spires of flowers minarets,
and trellises rose pantheons,
towered over by
proportions golden of an oak
the tenant of his own half acre.
The only proofs I know
of interstellar interference
with the fabric of this world,
the brutal concrete blots
that beat against the eye and soul
around the global slum,
a uniform sustained unpleasantness
from spirits
to whom the native art of Earth is alien.
What but a love to spread the ugly
could have brought them here
from the unrelieved square angles
and squat precincts of their hell
somewhere in space?

*a species rose   **a classic French rose

Way

They are changing the roads of the county.

Sispippiwa and Halt's Brothel and Billy Mountain
are roads where people went
where likely neither should have gone,
Duck Pond, Miller's Fault, Prison Farm Road
and two dozen different Christian Chapel Roads.

People went ways in error
without benefit of present time
and post-thought policy
that refigures the onery
into straight lace of x and y.

"Roads run wrong" say our leaders
who have studied at the right places
and who go each year
to do planetary planning in Hawaii.

They are changing the roads of the county.

A Rattlesnake History of Texas

Texas is dirt and rock
with still and running water.
The dirt is good part us;
aeons of us does it take to die and rot
and build the soil
that the winds somewhat blow
and rains sometimes wash away.

Our dirt it is
and that of other things that die here.
We have lived on it
a story of ambuscades
of necessary killing
in steady uneventful brief events of daily life and death,

till like storms from east
came stampedes of top-heavy bipeds,
Scots and Africans and Germans,
Irish and Czechs and Poles
and Anglos
over our dead bodies
taking serious care of themselves.

We warn before we bite
even impresarios who shake the odds
with tin leggings and with pistols,
and bipeds we bite seldom enough;
it's wasteful to envenomate
what you can't eat.

Their gear made a purpose not to rot
is covering Texas.
Soon there will be no dirt.

The Edge

Precise through trumpet and petal the light
bright yellow recollecting green
come daffodils crisp and statuesque
to sing the clearest melody of spring,
now unshakened by the wind
and backed with First Breath of Spring
whose blossoms lie dead wasps
around a vase upon a table.

The sly late-winter glory daffodil
desires
to drink the light when others sleep,
and feeds
when very few are hungry,
and lives
on the edge of everybody's space,
not in the way.

Rare Earth

Your arms my love
are they friendly
not just strong
but soft in kindliness
that does not change
that cannot hurt
but draws and comforts
a roundness of two
in a circle
of these arms.

Seventh Column*

Stubby are their heads;
life long underground,
has consumed their necks
up to the mouths
that twitch in foredelight
of ravening to come.
Betraying which
they leave ahead
hulks of bodies,
burnt out tanks
of periodic rising.
At work in solidarity they sing,
a million echoes of
a single raucous hum
that shivers up the stalks
of the green and living world.

*seven- or seventeen-year locusts

On Bishop Spong His Book

a rubric leaf of oak took wing
and smashed against a window pane
instantly itself a cardinal
and furious at the image (his own)
that had given such a blow

attached again to tree
denouncing and denying
virtuoso madness of the inner finch
against god and man and nature

Short Golden Curls in the Hopper Era
(S.G. 1933-1995 R.I.P)

I

His present narrow place recalls
a tiny dressing room at age fifteen
(in a modest pastel high school play)
without his shirt;
the girl stagehands and actresses
work the grease paint in.
Moth gardenias dart about a candle
the tips of their excited wings
lightly brush the flame
which dances more impressively
and for a while forgets the wings
but not the smell,
warm and not at all gardenia-like
of moving bodies.
Sweet now for him to think
easy to die in such a moment,
but as the culture's Baptist,
the bacchantes chaste
and the poet lacking license,
few boys contrive except in dreams
to die of a dozen dozen lovebites.

II

The later drama is his own,
the nightclub dark the colors deep
through a haze of perfumed smoke.
In each dim booth, beyond the bar,
lit by fire beneath the floor,
another and another woman waits for him

on padded seats no one ever sees
unless they're wet.
The moths are now camellias
smearing into purple and maroon.

III

In a booth just wide enough for two
with the girl he shares
a beginning of a notion
of lovers so entwined umbilically
a vein of either might irupt
And instead of bleeding
suck the other all way up.

IV

A committee of his women meet
in booths within the jukebox glow
to remember or invent
the cause of his undoing,
but they talk of clothes and lipstick.
the songs they hear are from
the barkeep's own collection
of operatic melancholy:

V

"The crossroads of humankind affords
only choices two in darkness
a Nothingness if not an All.
It was large and formless
like an argument out of Hegel
based if based at all on only two
points of fact: that he was living
and that he would die.

Maybe nothing has so fine a set of points,
and the closest he or any comes
is to thoughts about some thoughts
about some thoughts of life and death.
Little dayflies of the mind
in the flying generations
mutate without coherence,
and in the end not the head
nor the consumed consumer heart
recalls what the beginning was."

Wick's End

Our fathering slows
ekewise
to wick's end
and see does
last burn
bright as first?
In poor light
of bitter psalms
and in tents of Baal
(backsquints for the aghast)
is there yet mercy
and yet grace?
What care that empires
bud or canker
if past worth and weakly
we're two or three?

Half

The half candle celebration
catches an anemic eye
across a congregation
pocked like flack
with either/or beliefs.
But light is light,
there is no one-half light,
and a bit suffices
in the dark.

Fig Orchard

The Sweetness of Aunties

Even the affectionate
need exercise
in keeping fit
the cockles of the heart.
So aunts led me as a boy to think,
these muscle-glands of kindliness,
if kept in shape to be inflamed
produce the necessary enzymes for
good humor and good living.

Much of cockle exercise
is thought to be demeaning
(Even its advocates admit
it's "little'
and "unremembered")
like making cookies and listening,
telling stories and talking nonsense,
and teaching things like pulling up your socks.

The cockles of my uncles (all but one)
didn't seem to function well.
Their few efforts at body care
must have been
devoted to
maintenance of other parts.

I imagined some surgical
or chemical intervention
for uncles who are exercise-averse,
and supposed any day the Surgeon General
would mandate cockle insulation.

First Kisses (for Alice)

It was being thrown by the gods
into the girls' shower room
and waking asleep in the arms
of the very one of them I loved
who is weeping in charity

It was electric current
too hot for all fuses,
parents and teachers and priests,
small amperage unbelievers

It was learning all things at once
but better.

Sand and Sea

On the pale sunburned sand
the searing soles cry out
for waves just close enough
for stoicism.

China Wilson no doubt or Polar Scott
could go on and on,
or Solzhenitsyn,
with no water in sight
and no hope of flow
of respite after virtue,
reanimating respite for feet and men,
with cool plangency
and kisses after hot hard days,
soft couches,
grapes in two kinds,
and ebb
of pain.

It is no decadence or defeat
to be momently untested
and in no struggle,
resting for the sand tomorrow,
day well grounded in
the dreams of sea.

Our Daily Execution

The ribands of concrete row after row
lie heavy on the land,
unstopping highways,
each mile laid
by leveling mountains of money,
alongside which a very occasional jail.

On these concrete death rows
each day
one hundred
of our own residents or visitors
are done to death,
high old young low ugly cute
a singing superstar
a smart lawyer a stupid judge
teens of disparate dearness
to their parents
a drugdealer with golden curls and rings
driving his mom to church
a dead body in the trunk.

Too many, too often, too everywhere
to be news; the covered is what has not
been covered.

Where are the higher minded
in this arrant apathy,
where the initials of compassion,
the LPDS, Living Poets' Dissociation
for Suffering?

Ah, they too are roaring down the selfsame concrete rows
unslowed by the crosses on the roadside
and not noticing the gaps in streams of traffic
left by cars now crashed and bloody.

Capricious death, let us come to terms,
let the tender of heart learn
arithmetic.

Heaviest on us weighs
injudicial slaughter.

Poverty

(For David Robinson, R.I.P.)

Not always with us as before
the poor the wealth of Lawrence
are scarce in Rome and in the West,
by secular financing changed
into the class that likes to pay its bills,
and into the brazen new estate of funded victims.

The few remaining golden
misfortunate and poor
evade with more or less success
dragnets of the agencies of charity.

Where then is what's left of Lawrence's church
to find its human treasure?
Can it be mined from the global lode
of industrious consumers?

If the next make up
what this world lacks,
will these be mendicants
and charitable, faithful, hopeful, wise?
Did any prophet ever say so?

Present Love

My dearest Althea relent,
if you had slept with all
the singers you've admired
in one chorus so to speak
and later in a line of liaisons,
you would not be happier now.
A career of heavy turntable love--
the fast, the missionary 78s,
the 45s, small, crewcut, and kink,
the 33s and their thirds,
slow and elegant or smelly hip--
could that be recommended
by the maker
of the old Bang Olufsen?

What's nice is one
that still sweetly plays,
and wanting more just means escape
from boredom in the olde daunce.

In our embrace it's all one to me
that your mind gives pleasure to itself
thumbing through its collection of
vintage catalogs by Schwann.

Sugarplums

Aurelius, the mental vigor
of your bedridden love
suits well a time of virtual life
that seems likely to progress
up a cybered climax
where all that moves in sex
will be an eyelid.
If the raw world of body parts
lets you down
(your mother or another woman
could have told you)
the sirens in
the mind's bright sea
of accommodating ideal forms
may lull you into sleep,
in which unbitter you may learn
to abide with the gentler porn.
The rest is for the unillusioned.

A Cure for Love

Love is a kind of infantile paralysis
for which there's no vaccine.
The organ affected is the mind,
which tightens up around a single topic,
one's love or losing it or
getting more of it.
For two cases in a thousand
there is a cure:
finding another
with a mirror image
of the same disease.

The trouble is this recovery
is often followed by a wish
to be crippled yet again.

Against the Wind

Against the wind but for the light
against the cold against the dry,
a glass prism,
a warm and juicy and green house.

Out there, in space, maybe
Tom my mechanical guru hopes
there turns a happy planet
where beings with rather a human look
pique themselves upon their taste in tools,
not just how they work
but how they look and feel
to their owners, there, on this planet "Smithsonia,"
with only mechanical thoroughbreds,
beautiful in form
and sweetly useful,
devices one-off and not-to-be-improved-on,
whether made by skill, by grace, or by mistake.

Tom admires their choice of
certain old cars, cameras,
steam locomotives and printing machines,
horse-drawn farm tools and sailing ships.

The wonder for me
in this mechanic's Eden
is a National Greenhouse ('58)
of glass, and galvanized steel and redwood
and banks of hinged windows
that give by motion of handcranks
on worm gears in cast housings.

The housings leave generous space
for grease to ease great toothed arcs
that twist the long window shafts.
Just when it peaked in doing
all the duties of a greenhouse
its manufacture ceased, and in its place
came plastic condoms
some a half mile long,
needing tractors to stretch
the skin over quonset members.
Cheap to build,
they've made glass expensive new;
but the odd lover of glass prisms
can save an old house
from beneath the tracks
of Caterpillar Change,
who moves too fast to notice
he's not always going forward.

A labor of light, an effort of love, it is
to sort such crystals of tourmaline
(not just items of past sentiment,
having by chance been ours
in better and early times
but things that were truly right)
from the vast techno-terrain
where fashion and cheapness,
double agents of an insidious
multinational conspiracy,
extrude landfill new and improved.

Pity the Poor Devil

My agony column for the depraved
from editor's axe cannot be saved,
no advice needed
or truantly unheeded.
Can a man not make a living
advocating evil-giving?

Sin Is Too Hard a Topic

Sin is too hard a topic
for anyone but poets
who fail in every line and word
to burn them into heart and time.

What to do but commend it, sin,
and after hard nights
sing at breakfast
not at bath
sing filling up
not washing off.

Tasting Gumbo

admirari

the smell of Samaritans
the obscurity of light
the cunning of lips
the skin of trees
the splinters of intelligence
the whimsy of ecstasy
the playfulness of water
the abundance of unnecessary things
the loss of what was never ours
the shortness of long time
the electricity of synthesis
the ingeniousness of bores
the dedication of shrews
the stubbornness of zealots
the virility of error
the truffles of good taste
the custard of affection
the touch of love

The Under Art

No servant and no mastery
postmodern Michelangelo
is alien to scaffolding
by dint
of being ceiling-less.
It matters not a brush
the dare
is off not on the wall
without a floor,
free fall form
of antics by
dropping artist body
hopes a gesture
catches air
and throws him
for his moment
into stall.

Casualties

Sleepless, alert, at first light
we meet in glory,
challenged arms resplendent,
well reconnaissant
of the power of the other,
and brisk to encounter at sight.

Eager battalions
of erotic kindnesses
unleash
in forays of caresses,
corpsmen poised of charity
to comfort and restore.

Through the meridian
and long hot afternoon
of close engagement
one by one
good soldiers fall away
to cranky mercenaries
and bitter veterans.

Plate III: Seed of Pippin

My cold beginning
recollects forgetting
the excitement of begetting,
in seraphic sinning

that's tightened to
the bitter and the green
protected through
a taut osmotic skein
I grow
the green and bitter grow

into a translucence mellow
green flowing pink and yellow
the first and greatest quietest doing
the newing that precedes renewing
like the moon's relaxing
to wax aware of waxing

no heat can with matureness vie
for it all things grow cold and die
a redness gold
doughty round and bold
myriadal mad to shove
into rods and rounds of love

these swing me from the swinging air
squash upon a grounding care
of juiciness and tang
inebriative and erotic
giving every yin and yang
a polish and a final lick

The sweet tangles into rot
and delicious reek
dissolves the lot
to lightless sleep
that calls to me like mother trees
singing of the spring and bees.

For Robert Graves

The goddess nods to me that I can write
like Swift about her smelly parts.

By which I politely think she means
the flowery oils of hair,
fresh ocean salt of eye and nose
and apple tang of mouth.

It is my good luck to faint
overcome by milk and meadow
of her breasts

and in my sleep I learn:
the goddess has faults
but these are not to be found
on her sumptuous body.

Astral Love

In this our own bubble of space and time
mature in warm and skillful arms

watch out for asteroids and wrenches left outside
and those too in
and inside ourselves.

Is love impossible with watching out and in
and watching out and in impossible with love?

If we travel far enough
do they become one

or explode into vacuum
by wear and tear of living and loving long?

Justifacture

Scouring the earth of injustices
we tumble and fall
over the tumbled and fallen,
microbe or millionaire,
enchained or broken by
the tyranny of gravity.

What hope then but weightlessness,
or as near to it as possible
(our prophets the Cathars
and all emaciated saints
and latter-day witnesses in
anorexic clouds)
and what faith but hastened evolution
of hollow bones, tiny brains, and feathers

on marshy ground with weather by Microsoft?

Shadow Boxing

In the boxing ring of life
I count the blows that rain on head and heart.
As I try not to count the imaginary ones
I lose count
and begin to doubt who the opponent is
God, by which the crowd means the Big Guy that did it all to us,
or fate, faceless at least and at best an accident,
or my other self, a pitiless son-of-a-bitch;
he thinks the game is fixed and dangerous to win;
the host of victims ringside urge him on
their kind of champ.

I cheer myself not the less
and see in the referee's eyes misgivings
about partiality
and know in my corner there will be
towel, water, and a friend who pulls no punches.

Still Life

In Honor of the Birthday of the Painter Henryk Fantazos

I grow wrinkles on few acres far from sea.
As one part after
another of me fails,
I insist, 'I'm still me
the me I always was.'
Yet I notice I notice less,
my discourse ever about
the spirit of bodies.

A wisdom I seek
about beauty,
a woman's face the best that I can dream,
somewhat in dread this art my dream
may lack the very élan
of real women,
of mammals in the flesh?

An oversight by Linnaeus
not to call mammals "facials"?
These warm breast-lovers
are face givers and face takers
who whole books speak and read by looks,
and love to kiss and lick and nuzzle faces
more than any other places
except when cleaning or briefly mating
or more langorously nursing--
and in all three—cleaning, mating, nursing--
the eyes and nose and lips are players.

There is in a lovely face élan, that's so,
but a vibrant stillness too,
the liveliness of blood and wit
in a song
of the line.

A generosity in this face, and in art,
invites the world
to spend itself going over and again
the lively quiet
the shapes and colors
that the world dotes on,
teased into art by the panderer
Casanova and virtuoso eye.

To prove these questions
in a grainy mirror
I now strike poses,
and notice with care
my own indifferent features
that in my admiration begin to glow.

God knows what the old masters knew
but does their art suggest
objects bloom from kindly seeing,
waves or bits of light they send
echo back from eyes a grace?

Food for Thought

Instead of grace over oats in my bowl
I hear my mother years ago
scrape the bottom of the pot
and smell her husband (who owns the pot)
coughing out a blend
of one night's worth of booze and fags.
I see on the table an island for retreat,
it is an "oat,"
a single flake uncooked on an oilcloth sea,
dry and delicate and patterned,
product of a plant and a machine.
In my bowl I look for another single flake intact
in the warm and gooey mess.

This day in my present bowl
to ward away the recollected sound and smell and sight
I add raisins and butter, molasses and milk,
stuff for warm reflection on
grownups who railed against delights
that held me and them entranced.

And salt, too, I add,
in honor of my tribe that lived
on oats and salt to get to me.

Come, my precious ones,
forget the madeleines;
we'll dance the hey and the nonnie
to porridge and courage and life,
we'll dance the hey and the nonnie
to porridge and courage and life.

De-Poem?

I shoo from these lines the rash Houdinis
who would de-fuse
the little bombs of mind
that poems are,
and by legerdemain and props
pull them from a hat
of whirling bits of chaos
that are sometimes there and sometimes not,
where upon the poems and the chaos,
in generosity and pique,
dull sparkles of their own they shower.

Go in exile listen to
the length of the second vowel
and there encrypt the writing
on the tombs of the frantic souls
who first dreamed up
the five-year-plans
to rid the world of peasants.

Hard to kill, some things,
peasant, world, mind, poetry.

Song of the Line was designed by Dave Wofford of Horse & Buggy Press in Durham, North Carolina.

Charles Ellertson graciously provided his customized digital Bembo type which was used throughout, accompanied by a sparing use of Jenson Swash Italic. Larry Tseng provided valuable assistance in helping to optimize the scans of Henryk's engravings.

This first edition was offset printed by Thomson Shore on 80lb Mohawk Superfine text, a paper produced with electricity generated from wind power. The deluxe limited edition consists of the first ten copies of the edition accompanied by the complete suite of engravings. The limited edition copies, numbered 11–100 are accompanied by a single engraving.